PSALM 23

for *Women*

DISCOVER THE **ONE** WHO CARES FOR YOUR SOUL

JJ GUTIÉRREZ

ISBN: 9798853653559

Author JJ Gutierrez
Cover Design and Typesetting by JJ Gutierrez
Editing and Proofreading Katie Landers of www.integrityproofreading.com
Contact info: hello@jjgutierrezauthor.com

Dedication

This book is dedicated to the **women in my life** who spur me on in the LORD. There is no better friend than a friend who loves Jesus! Thank you for being that friend.

HELLO FRIEND,

This is Me!

Writer, teacher & ministry leader, but more importantly, an average gal with an amazing God & a deep love for Scripture. Accepting Jesus as my Savior over 28 years ago was the best decision of my life! Immediately I began studying the Bible. God's Word has become my guiding light, my strength and my joy. Nothing is more important to me than knowing God and studying Scripture. As a result, I've been growing & changing in miraculous ways.

But let's be honest...life is hard. It's filled with trials and temptations, but we are not alone. God's Word is there to lead and guide us. However, we must know the Bible to experience its power. As a woman, police wife, girl mom and homeschool mom, I understand the difference Scripture can make in daily life. That's why I'm compelled to create simple yet meaningful & rich Bible study workbooks. My heartfelt passion is to help everyday women and girls study the Bible so they can experience its power in their daily life too.

XO, JJ

Table of Contents

Introduction

When I was a teen girl I had a deep longing to be cared for. All my basic needs, like food, clothing, a place to live and an education were provided, but there was an ache for something more. Navigating the journey between childhood and adulthood created a new awareness inside me - I was more than my physical body. Intuitively I knew there was an inner part to my life. A part no one could see but lasts forever. A part more valuable than my visible frame. A part that made me who I am and allowed me to experience life and God in a meaningful way. That part of me is called my soul. And you have a soul too. In fact, every human being has a soul, and like our bodies, our souls need to be cared for.

But, what is a soul?

The soul is the immaterial aspect of you that consists of the mind, emotion and desire. Nelson's Illustrated Bible Dictionary defines the soul as, "*The inner life of a person, the seat of emotions, and the center of human personality.*" All of your desires, longings, thoughts, memories and feelings reside here. Jesus said the soul is worth more than gaining the whole world (Mark 8:36). The Bible explains the origin of our soul...it is when God breathed into man (Genesis 2:7). God gave us life when He gave us a soul. **Though you cannot see it, your soul is the most important part of you because it lasts forever** (Matthew 10:28).

The soul is the place where people can know and enjoy God. When we confess Jesus is Lord and believe in His death and resurrection, the soul is saved (Romans 10:9). It is within the soul a person feels connected to God and can experience His comfort, guidance and strength. With God our soul finds rest and peace even when life is troubling.

But the soul is also the place of great distress where unrest, anxiety and fear swell up. The location where sin begins and grows and lies are entertained. The hiding spot for sadness, loneliness and depression to take root. The place where enough is never enough and discontentment and complaining muddy and pollute the goodness of God. Left alone, the soul will soon fill with weeds leaving a person lost, confused and longing for relief. This is why the soul needs caretaking.

Many Christian women unknowingly focus on taking care of their outer life while neglecting their inner self...what clothes to wear, what products to buy to make you thinner, younger, smarter or prettier, what house to live in, what car to drive or what accomplishment will bring fulfillment. But even women who pay attention to their soul soon learn they are not equipped to provide for the soul's deepest, inmost needs. The soul needs tending. The soul needs a caretaker.

Introduction

Do you long for inner peace and rest? Do you crave comfort in the depths of your soul where no other human being can reach? When facing difficult decisions or a fork in the road, do you want guidance and direction? When life is scary and you can't see the road ahead do you yearn for courage and protection? Do you desire to be loved and cared for?

> *Stop for a moment and consider - What is your soul's deepest need today? Write your thoughts below.*

In this study you will dig deep into one of the most well-known and well-loved Psalms of all time. It's likely you are beginning this Bible study with some knowledge of this passage. Sunday school classes, Easter messages and funeral services are common places to hear the 23rd Psalm. However, I am going to ask you to set aside what you've heard and learned in the past and start afresh. **Let God's Word do the work of teaching you about The Shepherd. Let God's Word draw you close to the One who cares for your soul.**

This Bible study uses the **REAP Bible study method**: Reflect, Explore, Apply and Pray. The REAP Bible Study approach is an invitation to enter into a process of deep personal reflection while digging into the most transforming words of all time, God's Word. The four-step process is interwoven throughout the book to help you study the Bible in an engaging and meaningful way so you can uncover God's truth for yourself. The goal of each chapter is to *reap* - take in, gather and collect God's truth in your heart, and in return, it will produce a bounty of fruit in your life.

- **REFLECT**- Think deeply. Ponder one's heart. Look inward & respond.
- **EXPLORE**- Read & study God's Word. Analyze the truth.
- **APPLY**- Implications. Actions. What does this mean to my life?
- **PRAY**- In response to the study write your own ACTS Prayer.

My hope is at the end of this Bible study you'll gain more than head knowledge of Psalm 23. It's good to know about the Shepherd, but it's better to personally know the Shepherd! **May you develop a deep, heartfelt love and devotion for the Caretaker of your soul. May you find divine comfort, contentment, rest, protection and direction. May your soul declare with confidence, "*The LORD is MY shepherd; I have everything I need*"** (Psalm 23:1)!

Psalm 23

A psalm of David.

1 The Lord is my shepherd;
    I have all that I need.
2 He lets me rest in green meadows;
    he leads me beside peaceful streams.
3 He renews my strength.
  He guides me along right paths,
    bringing honor to his name.
4 Even when I walk
  through the darkest valley,
  I will not be afraid,
    for you are close beside me.
  Your rod and your staff
    protect and comfort me.
5 You prepare a feast for me
    in the presence of my enemies.
  You honor me by anointing my head with oil.
    My cup overflows with blessings.
6 Surely your goodness and unfailing love will
    pursue me all the days of my life,
    and I will live in the house of the Lord forever.

Psalm 23

GROUNDWORK

Groundwork is the process of preparing for a bigger work that is to come. It's the beforehand task that lays the foundation for the work ahead. Prior to taking an algebra class a pre-algebra class is required to learn the basic concepts. Without doing the groundwork ahead of time, mastering algebra will be difficult. The same holds true for Bible study. It's tempting to jump right into the text without laying the foundation for the text. The process of preparing to study any Scripture consists of identifying the literary genre, theme and author. Let's begin the groundwork for the Bible study of Psalm 23!

LITERARY GENRE

A genre is a category or grouping of writings with similar content, structure and mood. Understanding the genre of a text provides the reader with reading strategies. Psalm 23 is located in the book of Psalms. Psalms falls into the category of poetry and more specifically Hebrew poetry.

One of the most common characteristics of Hebrew poetry is imagery. Imagery illustrates the point the author is trying to convey with visually descriptive words or language that appeals to the senses. It can be literal or figurative; either way it allows the reader to vividly imagine the message the author is communicating.

There are two types of comparisions used in imagery - simile and metaphor. A simile teaches a truth by comparing it to something else. It includes the words *as* or *like* in the comparison and it's an indirect comparison.

1. An example of a **simile** is found in Psalm 42:1. Read the verse. Note below what is "as or like" what.

A **metaphor is** also a comparison, but it differs from a simile in one way...it does not include the words *as* or *like*. It's more direct because it ties the comparison more tightly together.

2. An example of a **metaphor** is found in Psalm 23:1. Read the verse. Note what two things are being compared to each other.

Psalm 23:1 is a metaphor. The author is not saying, *"The LORD is like a shepherd"* or *"As the LORD is a shepherd."* He is simply stating, *"The LORD is my shepherd"* (Psalm 23:1).

3. How does the difference between simile & metaphor impact how you view Psalm 23:1?

4. If Psalm 23:1 is implying the LORD is your shepherd what does it suggest you are?

When I was a child my friends and I would ask each other silly questions. One of the questions was, *"If you could be any animal which animal would you pick?"* My usual answer was a lion for its courage and strength or an owl for its wisdom. *How about you...what animal would you select?* While there are a variety of responses I've never heard anyone reply with, *"I'd like to be a sheep."* That's because a sheep's reputation is less than desirable. Sheep are helpless creatures who require a lot of guidance to survive and thrive. Yet, that is the creature David is implying we are in Psalm 23. We are sheep because the LORD is our shepherd.

5. Look at the list of characteristics in the box. Put a checkmark by any characteristics you personally identify with. Ask the Lord to become your shepherd in those areas of your life.

6. Open your Bible and read Psalm 23. What images come to your mind as you look over this passage?

7. Poetry is known for evoking emotion. What emotions do you feel when you read Psalm 23?

Characteristics of Sheep

- Fearful & timid
- Easily spooked
- Defenseless
- Run when scared
- Easily led astray
- Have mob mentality
- Are easy prey
- Stubborn
- Panic with uncertainty
- Needy
- Gullible
- Can't clean themselves
- Can't get up if on their back
- Emotionally complex
- Highly social animals
- Depressed in isolation
- Self medicate by eating plants
- Follow one another
- Face jealousy amongst the flock
- Irritated by small things
- Restless when thirsty
- Directionally challenged

THEME

Poetry is often organized into stanzas. Stanzas are groupings of lines that might look simliar in size. Stanzas consist of verses and verses may repeat thoughts in multiple ways. All of the thoughts support one main point. The main point is the theme.

1. Look back at Psalm 23. What is the main point that all the verses support? Can you name the theme in a few words? Write it below.

AUTHOR

David, one of the greatest characters in the Bible, is the author of Psalm 23. He is the only person referred to as a *man after God's own heart* (1 Samuel 13:14). David is credited with writing 73 of the 150 psalms. Many of David's psalms were laments revealing his darkest moments of fear, depression and the devastating effects of sin. But he also wrote psalms of praise and thanksgiving. Often David declared his confident trust and unwavering faith in God regardless of the visible circumstances he faced. He was a shepherd boy, a musician, a warrior and Israel's greatest king.

1. Look up the Bible verses below. What do you learn about who David is?

   - 1 Samuel 16:1, 13-14

   - 1 Samuel 16:18

   - 1 Samuel 17:14-15

   - 1 Samuel 17:34-35 (in some Bible versions David refers to himself as "your servant")

- 1 Samuel 17:48-50

- 2 Samuel 5:3-4

- Acts 13:22

2. After reading about David, why was he equipped and able to write such a powerful metaphor in the Psalm comparing his relationship with God to a shepherd and a sheep?

The exact date when David penned Psalm 23 is unknown. David could have written the Psalm as a shepherd boy, after he defeated Goliath, when he was on the run from Saul, during his reign as king, in his downfall due to sin or toward the end of his life. No matter when it was written, Psalm 23 expresses David's personal faith, trust and confidence in God. **His words are applicable to believers today and they continue to bring comfort and strength to those who read it, hear it, study it and/or memorize it.**

Congratulations!

You have completed the groundwork for Psalm 23. By identifying the literary genre, the theme and the author you've laid the foundation for the text and you are ready to begin a more meaningful study of one of the greatest psalms of all time.

"The Lord is my shepherd;
I have all that I need."

PSALM 23:1

Psalm 23

THE SHEPHERD OF YOUR SOUL

Everyone has the same essential needs to sustain life. Basic but critical things like food, clothing, a place to live and an income. Without such things you'd find yourself hungry, cold, naked and homeless. Missing any one of life's necessities surely initiates a deep longing resulting in feelings of lack, want and discontentment. But even when all of life's basic requirements are met a person might still have feelings of lack and want. These feelings of discontentment come from a person's soul. The soul has needs too.

A Christian woman might think she's immune from feelings of want or lack. But even the strongest woman of faith can fall into the trap of believing worldly things like material items, prominence, talent, wealth, beauty or job success will satisfy the needs of the soul. She might think, "When this happens or I get that, then I will be happy." However, having all of these things can still leave an emptiness inside. Contentment seems impossible because deep in the heart the soul craves something the world cannot provide. It desires a Caretaker.

Psalm 23 provides a beautiful illustraion of David's relationship with God. He compared it to that of a shepherd and a sheep. Believe it or not you have a lot in common with sheep. Sheep need rest, direction, protection and comfort. Without the shepherd they become agitated, afraid and are prone to wander or follow the wrong sheep. The presence of the shepherd and the sound of his voice restores peace and contentment. The shepherd meets all of the sheep's needs and they lack for nothing. And just like sheep require a shepherd so your soul needs one too. **The Shepherd David spoke so personally and powerfully about over 3,000 years ago is the same Shepherd who wants to care for your deepest needs today.** When He is your shepherd your soul will be satisfied.

> ## SOUL NEED #1: CONTENTMENT
>
> **Traits:** Satisfied. At ease. Free of worry. Free of want.
>
> **Struggle:** When _____, then I'll be satisfied.
>
> **Truth:** Right here, right now the Shepherd satisfies the soul.

WHEN/THEN

Contentment is an overall feeling of satisfaction, ease and well-being. Not lacking or wanting, instead resting assured that what one has is enough. A common struggle with contentment is when/then thinking. When/then thoughts sound like this - *when* I get a car, new clothes, a new house, then I will be happy. However, contentment centered on when/then is faulty thinking because when the worldly want is fulfilled, happiness is short lived and the soul returns to longing for something else. It's a never ending cycle leaving a girl chasing inner fulfillment that can never be satisfied by outward things.

1. Look at the list of Contentment Struggles on the next page. Can you relate to any of the when/then statements? Put a check mark next to all that apply to you.

2. Can you think of another when/then a girl might think? Fill in the blank.

When _____ , then I'll be _____

3. Why do you think when/then thoughts will never lead to lasting contentment?

Contentment Struggles

- When I get married , then I'll be happy
- When I'm at my ideal weight, then I'll be content
- When my family has no conflict , then I'll be at ease
- When I have children, then I'll be fulfilled
- When I get a new car, then I'll be glad

- When I get my dream job, then I'll be satisfied
- When my kids grow up, then I'll be happy
- When I have no more debt, then I'll be pleased
- When I retire, then I'll be complete
- When I get invited, then I'll be joyful

MEET THE SHEPHERD

In the first verse of Psalm 23 David presents a powerful statement, *"The LORD is my shepherd."* Not just any ordinary shepherd but the Shepherd who provides for all the needs of His people. With His provision, the soul lacks for nothing. But who is this Shepherd that quenches the soul's deepest longings and meets the inmost needs of human beings? Let's explore the Scriptures to find out more about who He is.

1. Open your Bible and read Psalm 23:1. Write the missing word on the line below. What do you notice about *this* word that is different than the other text in the verse?

"The _____ is my shepherd; I have everything I need."

Psalm 23:1

In the Bible when LORD is in all capital letters it means the Hebrew name for God - Yahweh. The English translation is Jehovah. Jehovah means the self-existing God who needs nothing outside Himself to complete Himself. The never-changing, always-present, everlasting-God!

2. Read Exodus 3:13-15. What else do you learn about God's name Yahweh?

David pairs God's name Yahweh with shepherd. You could say, **"Yahweh is my shepherd."**

3. From the verses below, what do you learn about The Shepherd? Draw a line from the verse to the quality of a shepherd listed in the box. Not all qualities will have a verse.

- Psalm 78:52

- Isaiah 40:11

- Jeremiah 31:10

- Ezekiel 34:11-12

- John 10:10

- I Peter 2:25

Qualities of a Shepherd

- Cares for the flock
- Provides food & water
- Searches & rescues lost sheep
- Protects the sheep
- Tends to the sick
- Guides & leads the flock
- Defends against enemies
- Gathers the sheep
- Oversees the sheep (guardian)
- Strengthens the weak
- Puts the needs of the sheep first
- Sacrifices his life for the sheep

4. From the Scriptures you looked up and the list above what does your soul need most today? Why?

5. What verb tense do you find in the first half of Psalm 23:1? Write 3 words to describe how it affects the meaning.

6. Write down all the pronouns found in Psalm 23:1. What insight do these pronouns provide about this Psalm?

LACK FOR NOTHING

In the second part of Psalm 23:1 David declares all his needs are met. The ESV version of the Bible states it this way, *"I shall not want"* and the Amplified version says, *"I shall not lack."* David isn't claiming all his personal wants and desires are fulfilled. Instead, David trusted God to supply his true needs which are the deeper needs of his soul. This verse could be read as *"God is enough. I need nothing else to be content. My soul is at rest."*

7. Read the following verses. What do these verses say about the people who lack nothing?

   • Psalm 34:9-10

   • Matthew 6:31-33

8. The Scriptures say people who lack nothing are those who seek the Lord (Jeremiah 29:13), trust in God (Proverbs 3:5-6), fear Him (Proverbs 14:2) and live in obedience to His Word (Luke 11:28). Do you do these things? Rate yourself in the areas below.

	Always		50% of the time		Never
Seek God	1	2	3	4	5
Trust God	1	2	3	4	5
Fear God	1	2	3	4	5
Live Rightly	1	2	3	4	5

9. What is one area you need to work on? What is one thing you can do to improve it?

IS THE LORD YOUR SHEPHERD?

David was well acquainted with tending sheep. As a shepherd boy, he learned how to care for the needs of the flock. He understood what it meant to provide, guide and protect them. It's from this viewpoint David relates to God. David's statement about his relationship to God as his shepherd wasn't about community or many people...it was singular. He said, "*My shepherd*"...not, "*Our shepherd*" or "*The people of God's shepherd,*" but his very own personal shepherd.

Enjoying the benefits of the Shepherd's care and provision and finding soul contentment begins with a personal relationship with Jesus. *Have you received Jesus as your Savior?* If Jesus is not your personal Savior, today your soul can experience inner peace and contentment through forgiveness and new life in Jesus. Please turn to page 57 to learn how to follow Jesus.

Christian women who trust the Shepherd can still experience times of want. During times of wanting, lacking or needing, here are four questions that can help you navigate the want in your heart.

4 Questions To Ask in Times of Want

1. Is what I want what I really need?
2. Is what I want good for me?
3. Is the timing right for what I want?
4. Is what I want in line with what God wants for me?

1. Think of a want you currently or recently have and answer the "4 Questions to Ask in Times of Need." What do your answers tell you about your want?

    My want or need:

       1.

       2.

       3.

       4.

ACTS PRAYER

After each Bible study you will be prompted to write an ACTS prayer. This four-step prayer method includes adoration, confession, thanksgiving and supplication. A description of each step is below. **As you write your prayer consider what you have learned about Psalm 23.**

For example: **Praise** God for being your Shepherd. **Confess** a tendency to seek contentment in worldly things and when/then thinking. **Thank** God for His provision. **Ask** God to give you a heart of contentment.

Dear Lord,

Adoration
Give praise, honor, and glory to God for He is Lord over all.

I praise you because...

Confession
Repent, come clean & admit your sins, ask for forgiveness.

Forgive me for...

Thanksgiving
Recount your blessings & thank God for all He has done.

Thank you for...

Supplication
Make your requests, both for yourself and others. Ask God for what you need.

My requests are...

In Jesus' Name, Amen

"He lets me rest in green meadows;
He leads me beside peaceful streams.
He renews my strength."

PSALM 23:2-3

Psalm 23

HE PROVIDES REST

For some women bedtime is difficult. Whether it's the Netflix series enticing her to watch one more episode, the baby crying throughout the night, the cupcakes she forgot to bake for tomorrow's potluck or the hormonal changes of the female body, getting into bed and falling deep asleep can be a challenge. A girl might find herself wishing for more hours of the day or that her body would require less sleep. But sleep is good and making oneself lie down to rest is necessary. Sleep is critically important to rejuvenating and strengthening every part of a woman's body. The body needs downtime so you make yourself lie down to sleep.

Just like the physical body needs rest so does your soul because your soul is impacted by life's challenges. Certainly, you are aware that life isn't all butterflies and cupcakes. Most likely you've experienced several difficult situations by now. Maybe painful relationships, maybe not getting the job or enduring loss, financial hardship or sickness and disease. Let's be honest. Hard times happen and during difficulties your soul can become weary, tired, defeated or discouraged.

Thankfully, we are not on our own to fix our weary souls. If so, we'd look to worldly devices, material items or human wisdom for solutions only to find out they don't work. In Psalm 23, David paints a picture of the perfect answer to a weary soul. Like a shepherd provides green pastures and still waters for his sheep to rest, so God provides a place for you. After all, who is better equipped to take care of you than the Shepherd? The One who loves you beyond measure and knows your inner needs more than you do furnishes the green pastures and still waters that will satisfy your soul.

> ## SOUL NEED #2: REST
>
> **Traits:** Lie down. Relax. Refresh.
>
> **Struggle:** Don't lie down easily. Insist on staying active.
>
> **Truth:** The Shepherd provides the place where rest is possible.

STRUGGLING TO LIE DOWN

REST is the first provision the Shepherd provides for His sheep. In our culture today it's easy to discount the importance of resting but rest refreshes the body and soul. However, sheep, like humans, do not lie down easily. Sheep have needs that must be met before lying down is possible. They require green pastures where there is safety, tranquility, nutrition and most importantly the presence of their shepherd. A good shepherd knows his flock must rest, so he lovingly makes them lie down by supplying all they need to relax. However, the "making" is not forceful. He brings the sheep to the green pasture but the sheep have to decide to partake. There are many reasons Christians do not enjoy the rest God gives...worry, fear, distractions, annoyances, unconfessed sin or a distant relationship with God. Any one of these can keep your soul from the rest it desperately desires.

1. Sheep need to be free of hunger and thirst before they can lie down and rest. What do you need to be free of so you can lie down at night to rest?

2. There are many reasons a person's soul becomes weary and restless. What is something that keeps your soul from resting?

EXAMINE CLOSELY

At the beginning of Psalm 23, David confidently declares, *"The LORD is my shepherd; I have everything I need"* (Psalm 23:1). The remainder of the Psalm supports why David lacks nothing. As you dig into the next section of Psalm 23 ask God to help you understand how He meets your needs so you can be as sure as David when you say, *"The LORD is my shepherd."*

Look at the Scripture and answer the questions below.

"He lets me rest in green meadows; He leads me beside peaceful streams. He renews my strength..." Psalm 23:2-3 NLT

1. Underline any words that create a mental image. What pictures come to mind when you read this verse? Make notes below.

2. What human needs are represented in this verse?

3. Circle all the personal pronouns. Who are the personal pronouns referring to?

4. Put a box around the verbs. How do these verbs inform you about what is happening?

5. Summarize what you learned about the Shepherd.

GREEN PASTURES & PEACEFUL STREAMS

Psalm 23:2 is a beautiful depiction of sheep resting in green pastures near peaceful streams. It's the ideal place for sheep to be refreshed. Early in the morning when the grass is still wet with dew the shepherd leads his flock to eat and drink. They eat until their hunger is satisfied. Then, with a full tummy, the sheep are able to lie down and rest. A shepherd with a flock resting is a shepherd whose sheep are content because he has supplied their needs.

As you complete the remainder of the Explore section consider this: Are you satisfied in God's green pastures near His peaceful streams? Is your soul resting in the Shepherd's care or is your soul restless, wandering and hungry?

3 WAYS THE SHEPHERD LEADS YOU TO REST:
FAITH, FEED & TRUST

FAITH AND REST: God made the perfect place for your soul to find eternal rest and His name is Jesus. Through faith in Him your soul enters into God's green pastures. You can't earn, work for or buy peace with God. It simply must be accepted by faith. The soul can rest from working for salvation when it rests in the finished work of Christ on the cross. The world will say, *"Do more, get more, strive harder,"* but the Bible tells us Jesus is all we need.

6. What does a person need to do to find soul rest? Look up the verses below. Try to write your answer in one or two words.

   • John 3:16

   • John 5:24

   • Romans 10:13

FEED & REST: Sometimes a lack of rest comes from a hungry soul. Just like the body needs food so does the deep inner part of you. Many women try to fill their empty souls with fleshly things like material items, accomplishments or over consuming social media, Netflix or ice cream. The result is a restless, uneasy and very unsatisfied soul. To satiate soul hunger the soul needs to feed on the Word of God.

7. What do you learn about food for your soul (God's Word) from the verses below? Draw a line to the correct answer.

1. Job 23:12   With God's Word I'll never be hungry or thirsty again.

2. Jeremiah 15:16   More than daily bread, I treasure your words.

3. Matthew 4:4   God's Words are my joy and my heart's delight.

4. John 6:35   More than bread, I need the Word of God.

TRUST & REST: A soul at rest doesn't mean a life without trials and hardship. Jesus said, *"Here on earth you will have many trials and sorrows. But take heart, because I have overcome the world"* (John 16:33). During life's storms inner rest is possible by trusting in God's promises. When the soul is struggling with feeling alone, scared, lost or worried lying down to sleep can be a challenge. Comfort comes through relying on, and trusting in, God to follow through. God is faithful to keep His promises (Hebrews 10:23).

8. From these Scriptures what promises can you count on? Why does each promise give your soul rest?

- Deuteronomy 31:8

- Isaiah 40:31

- James 1:5

- I John 1:9

A Soul at Rest

- Has faith in Jesus
- Reads & feeds on the Word of God
- Trusts in God's Promises

A soul resting in God's green pastures near His peaceful streams is one whose faith is in Jesus, who reads & feeds on the Word of God and who trusts in God's promises. The Shepherd has given you everything you need, but you must live in His provision.

Jesus Invites You to Rest

> *"Come to me, all who labor and are heavy laden, and I will give you rest. Take my yoke upon you, and learn from me, for I am gentle and lowly in heart, and you will find rest for your souls. For my yoke is easy, and my burden is light." Matthew 11:28-30*

HOW HAVE YOU BEEN SLEEPING LATELY?

Many times sleepless nights stem from a weary, uneasy or anxious soul. A girl might unintentionally try to solve all her problems during the twilight hours. But worry accomplishes nothing while leaving the body and soul exhausted. Recalling God's promises while lying in bed can calm and refocus the soul. An excellent verse to call upon in the wee hours of the night is Matthew 11:28-30.

1. What promise do you find in Matthew 11:28-30?

One method of recalling God's promises is to visualize them. You can do this by imagining the verse in your mind. Let's practice with Psalm 23:2 and Matthew 11:28-30. Picture yourself sitting in a green pasture. Hear the sound of a peaceful stream. See Jesus with His arms extended. He is inviting you to come and rest with Him. As you sit with Him, unload all your burdens by telling Him your worries, cares, fears, hurts and frustrations. Everything causing your soul distress. Then watch, as Jesus, the Shepherd of your soul, takes your burdens and gives you peace and rest. Linger there for a while. Notice the enjoyment you feel being with your Shepherd, the One who cares for your soul.

Next time you have trouble sleeping repeat this process and let Jesus, your Shepherd, give your soul rest.

ACTS PRAYER

As you write your prayer consider what you have learned about Psalm 23.

Dear Lord,

Adoration

Give praise, honor, and glory to God for He is Lord over all.

> I praise you because...

Confession

Repent, come clean & admit your sins, ask for forgiveness.

> Forgive me for...

Thanksgiving

Recount your blessings & thank God for all He has done.

> Thank you for...

Supplication

Make your requests, both for yourself and others. Ask God for what you need.

> My requests are...

In Jesus' Name, Amen

"...He guides me along right paths, bringing honor to his name."

PSALM 23:3

Week 4

Psalm 23

HE PROVIDES DIRECTION

Do you remember the day you got your driver:s license? Leaving the Department of Motor Vehicles with the legal right to drive is an exciting feeling. Even better is jumping in the car and cruising down the road with the music playing and the windows down. Driving places is part of a woman's life and now-a-days drivers need not fear getting lost. GPS navigation is like a trusted friend, but there was a time when GPS navigation did not exist. Depending on your age you might remember trying to find your way to new destinations the old fashioned way...writing the directions on a piece of paper or using a physical map. Missing a turn, not seeing a street name or unknowingly heading the wrong direction was a real possibility. Without GPS to pinpoint the way, a girl could easily become lost or end up in the wrong place, maybe even a dangerous place.

Thankfully, built into every smartphone is a navigation system. With a few strokes of the finger the system will guide you turn by turn to your desired location. It's comforting to know you can get where you need to go without worry or fear as long as you follow the route. Just like driving to physical locations requires direction, so your soul needs direction too. Without a guide to show the way, you can easily get lost by following the world's ways or by letting curiosity about sinful things lead you astray. **Thankfully, you have a personal guide who lovingly directs your soul toward the right pathway of life.** He is the Shepherd, the One who made you and the One who knows the best way for you to go. When you follow Him, He will surely bring you safely to your destination.

SOUL NEED #3: DIRECTION

Traits: Navigate which way to go. Pathway. Route. Guide.

Struggle: Don't want to follow. Stubborn. Insists on own way.

Truth: The Shepherd provides personal direction & it's right & good.

DIRECTIONALLY CHALLENGED

David continues comparing his relationship with God to that of a shepherd and his sheep by stating, *"He guides me along right paths..."* (Psalm 23:3). David understood sheep are directionally challenged creatures. They have a tendency to wander off and get lost, to follow a sheep who's gone astray or to walk the same worn out, rutty road over and over again. Like sheep, Christian women are vulnerable to losing all sense of direction too. Look at the three scenarios below.

Woman One

This woman didn't mean to wander away from God but the worries and cares of life have consumed her mind and heart. Without realizing it, she walked away from God to follow her own plan. Her own way led her far away from the Shepherd & the distance has left her feeling lost and alone..

Woman Two

This woman struggles with worldly temptation.. The shiny new thing, cultural influences or sinful desires easily lead her to poor choices..This woman says to herself, *"I can dabble in this and still maintain my Christian life."* Before she realizes it, she's been led astray. Following her fleshly desires resulted in unfollowing God.

Woman Three

This woman wants to follow Jesus but she struggles to make new habits. She likes her way of life. It's familiar. It's known. It's predictable. And it's hers. She continues to walk the same roads over and over again, even pathways that aren't healthy or good. This woman is trapped by her own self-deception.

1. Which of the the three women above do you most closely relate to? Why?

EXAMINE CLOSELY

At the beginning of Psalm 23, David confidently declares, *"The LORD is my shepherd; I have everything I need"* (Psalm 23:1). The remainder of the Psalm supports why David lacks nothing. As you dig into the next section of Psalm 23 ask God to help you understand how He meets your needs so you can be as sure as David when you say, *"The LORD is my shepherd."*

Look at the Scripture and answer the questions below.

"...He guides me along right paths, bringing honor to his name."

Psalm 23:3 NLT

1. Underline any words that create a mental image. What pictures come to mind when you read this verse? Make notes below.

2. What human needs are represented in this verse?

3. Circle all the personal pronouns. Who are the personal pronouns referring to?

4. Put a box around the verbs. How do these verbs inform you about what is happening?

5. Summarize what you learned about the Shepherd.

HE GUIDES ME ALONG RIGHT PATHS

Sheep can't be driven or forced to go. They must be gently and lovingly led. A good shepherd points out the way, he leads from the front and he travels along with the sheep. As the overseer of the flock, the shepherd guides the sheep with his voice. The sheep know what his voice sounds like and they can distinguish his voice from other voices. When the sheep follow their shepherd's voice they can rest assured they are on the right path. Even when the road is rough and dry they can trust the shepherd. He always takes them to places of rest and restoration. Places away from danger. Places of safety and peace.

6. Look up John 10:25-27 and answer the questions below.

   • Who is the personal Shepherd of God's sheep?

   • What do God's sheep know and do?

7. **A girl can know Jesus but still choose not to follow Him in her daily life.** Hearing and following His voice is a matter of the heart. Read Psalm 25. What do you learn about the heart of the woman who looks to the Shepherd to guide and lead her? Draw a line from the verse to the correct heart attitude.

   1. Psalm 25:4   A heart that is humble.

   2. Psalm 25:5   A heart that fears God.

   3. Psalm 25:9   A heart that waits on & hopes in God.

   4. Psalm 25:10   A heart with eyes on God.

   5. Psalm 25:14   A heart that asks God.

   6. Psalm 25:15   A heart that obeys God.

8. Look at the list of heart attitudes from question 7 and write the one you need to work on the most. Ask God to change your heart in that area.

9. Look up the the verses below and note the two primary ways
   God guides and directs believers today.

   - John 16:13

   - Psalm 119:105

Soul Direction

**WHEN YOU NEED TO KNOW
WHICH WAY TO GO**

READ YOUR BIBLE & ASK THE HOLY
SPIRIT TO SHOW YOU THE WAY

BRINGING HONOR TO HIS NAME

In Psalm 23, David called God by His personal name Yahweh, also known as LORD. God's names reveal His character and nature to us. Yahweh means the right here, right now God who has always existed and never changes. David's confidence that God would lead him along right paths *bringing honor to His name* was grounded in the character of Yahweh. He knew his well-being was closely connected to Yahweh's reputation. Yahweh is a faithful shepherd who takes care of His sheep and keeps His promises. He is motivated to personally lead His sheep on the best path for each one individually because what is best for them also honors His name.

Trusting other people to follow through with their promises has the potential to end in disappointment. However, trusting in God will never fail you. You can count on Him to be true to His character.

10. Why can you trust God to lead your soul in right paths for His name sake?

    - Psalm 145:13

    - 2 Timothy 2:13

    - Hebrews 10:23

11. Go back and re-read Psalm 23:1. As you follow the Shepherd, what does the Shepherd promise to give you?

God's faithfulness accompanies your soul as you walk His right roads. As you rely on the Shepherd to lead you, He is glorified. When you make difficult but right decisions, when you keep your ears attuned to the Shepherd's voice when other voices are vying for your attention or when you travel through inner pain with steadfast hope, God's name is honored and lifted high. He is faithful to "*bring honor to His name*" (Psalm 23:3).

WHEN YOU ARE ON THE WRONG PATH

At the beginning of this chapter you were presented with three different women who walked away from the right path (see page 27). Most Christian women can relate to all three situations at different times in their lives. Maybe you are facing one of those situations right now. **What should a girl do when she finds herself on the wrong path?**

The answer is so simple it's almost too good to be true! Simply turn back to the Shepherd. The Bible says, "Once you were like sheep who wandered away. But now you have turned to your Shepherd, the Guardian of your souls" (I Peter 2:25). **To turn means to change direction, reverse or go back.** The book of James provides great insight on how to turn to God. James says, "Come close to God and He will come close to you" (James 4:8). Below are three ways to draw near to God. Your soul can get back on track when you do the following -

Humble Yourself:

Humble Yourself (James 4:7) - humble yourself by realizing God knows what's best for your life. Surrender your plans to His.

Resist the Devil:

Resist the Devil (James 4:7) - Satan doesn't want you to turn back to God. Refuse listening to his lies. Listen to your Shepherd's voice calling you back.

Wash Your Hands:

Wash Your Hands (James 4:8) - Confess your sins and receive forgiveness. Live rightly. Wholeheartedly follow Jesus.

1. When you feel far away from God are you quick to humble yourself, resist the devil and wash your hands (confess)? Why or why not?

ACTS PRAYER

As you write your prayer consider what you have learned about Psalm 23.

Dear Lord,

Adoration

Give praise, honor, and glory to
God for He is Lord over all.

I praise you because...

Confession

Repent, come clean & admit
your sins, ask for forgiveness.

Forgive me for...

Thanksgiving

Recount your blessings & thank
God for all He has done.

Thank you for...

Supplication

Make your requests, both for
yourself and others. Ask God for
what you need.

My requests are...

In Jesus' Name, Amen

"Even when I walk through the darkest valley, I will not be afraid, for you are close beside me. Your rod and your staff protect and comfort me."

PSALM 23:4

Psalm 23

HE PROVIDES COMFORT

When you were a little girl were you afraid of the dark? Maybe, as an adult, that frightening feeling still happens. Actually, it's pretty normal for people of all ages to experience some fear of darkness because without any light vision is impaired. Not being able to see what's across the room or what's right in front of you is disorienting and can produce panic and alarm. Fears of unseen dangers manage to grow out-of-control as the imagination runs wild with thoughts of something or someone lurking in the darkness. It is the sound of a familiar voice that calms your soul. Hearing the voice brings instant comfort because it's evidence you're not alone. Your husband, a family member or someone you know and trust is with you. Knowing someone is with you relieves all your fears.

Like people, sheep have problems in the darkness too. It's because sheep lack good vision and the darkness intensifies their inability to see well. Also, sheep are easily frightened by sudden sounds and movements. They know lions, foxes and wolves prowl around at night looking for a meal. Whether it's actually nighttime or the shepherd is leading the flock through a dark valley, sheep are afraid. It is the shepherd's presence and his voice that strengthens and reassures the sheep for the journey.

Darkness doesn't only occur in physical places lacking sunlight or a lamp. It can also happen deep within a person's soul. In Psalm 23:4, David uses the metaphor "darkest valley" to describe difficult days when the soul is weighed down by grief, fear, depression or anxiety. During dark and troublesome times becoming afraid is a natural response, but you need not fear. David said, "I will not be afraid, for you are close beside me" (Psalm 23:4). He knew his soul was not alone; the Shepherd was with him and the Shepherd is with you too. It's His close presence that provides your soul comfort in the dark valleys of life.

SOUL NEED #4: COMFORT

Traits: Encouragement. Relief. Assurance during scary times.

Struggle: When life is frightening, easily stuck in fear & discouragement.

Truth: The Shepherd provides comfort to get through scary times.

STUCK IN THE DARK VALLEY

In Psalm 23:4, David wrote, *"Even when I walk through the darkest valley, I will not be afraid."* He didn't say, *"Even when I am staying, building a nest or taking up permanent residence in the darkest valley"* because **dark valleys are meant to be traveled through not lived in**. Yet, like so many people, Christian women can find themselves stopping, unpacking and making a home. But why would anyone choose to remain in the dark valleys of life? The root cause can be summed up in two powerful words - fear and discouragement.

n the darkness, fear whispers in one ear, "You're going to fail, get rejected, they don't like you, you are all alone or you just don't have the strength," While discouragement is in the other ear saying, "It's hopeless, impossible...might as well give up." All of this inner noise quickly drowns out the voice of God leaving a woman's soul stranded in the darkness. She might be tempted to believe the dark valley is her permanent position in life. But the Shepherd never intended for His sheep to get stuck...He intends to lead her through.

Dark valleys are a fact of life. And it's frightening when you cannot see beyond what's happening or you don't know how the situation will work out. **But God's way is nonstop, one-way, through the valley.** The best news is with the Shepherd guiding you, you're sure to arrive safe and sound on the other side.

1. Have you ever felt stuck in a dark valley of life? What thoughts and feelings kept you trapped?

EXAMINE CLOSELY

At the beginning of Psalm 23, David confidently declares, *"The LORD is my shepherd; I have everything I need"* (Psalm 23:1). The remainder of the Psalm supports why David lacks nothing. As you dig into the next section of Psalm 23 ask God to help you understand how He meets your needs so you can be as sure as David when you say, *"The LORD is my shepherd."*

Look at the Scripture and answer the questions below.

"Even when I walk through the darkest valley, I will not be afraid, for you are close beside me. Your rod and your staff protect and comfort me." Psalm 23:4 NLT

1. Underline any words that create a mental image. What pictures come to mind when you read this verse? Make notes below.

2. What human needs are represented in this verse?

3. Circle all the personal pronouns. Who are the personal pronouns referring to?

4. Put a box around the verbs. How do these verbs inform you about what is happening?

5. Summarize what you learned about the Shepherd.

MIDWAY SHIFT

Psalm 23:4 not only marks the half-way point of this psalm but David's voice shifts.

6. What pronoun is David using when referring to God in Psalm 23:2-3?

7. What pronoun is David using when referring to God in Psalm 23:4-6?

8. What does the change in how Daivd refers to God indicate?

David's words shift from talking *about* the Shepherd to talking *to* the Shepherd. When David is in green pastures he tells about God but when David is in the dark valley he turns and talks directly to God. This illustration depicts a shepherd not far away but one who is up close and personally involved during the trials, hardships and challenges of his sheep.

9. When your soul feels overshadowed by fear, anxiety, uncertainty or difficulty do you turn and talk directly to God? Why or why not?

Soul Comfort

IS ANCHORED IN

- God's Presence
- God's Protection (the rod)
- God's Guidance (the staff)

COMFORT IN HIS PRESENCE

Read Isaiah 43:1-3.

10. From Isaiah 43:1, how personally does God know you?

11. From Isaiah 43:2, what does it say will happen when you go through deep waters, rivers of difficulty or fires of oppression?

COMFORT FROM THE ROD & STAFF

Psalm 23:4 says, *"Your rod and your staff protect and comfort me."* Look at the chart on this page to learn more about the rod and the staff.

12. Why would sheep find comfort in knowing their Shepherd has these two instruments in His hands?

13. Read the verses below. Which verse is an example of the shepherd using a rod or a staff? Why? (see Rod & Staff chart for help)

   - I Samuel 17:34-35

   - Matthew 18:12-14

Rod & Staff

THE ROD

- A symbol of God's power
- A club like weapon
- Used to protect sheep
- Used to fight off & kill wild animals
- Used to keep sheep away from predators

THE STAFF

- A symbol of God's grace
- A long, slender stick with a hook
- Used to guide sheep
- Used to pull sheep back from harm
- Used to bring a sheep close to the shepherd

14. Think of a current or recent trial or challenge. Which instrument (rod or staff) brings you the most comfort? Why?

David paints a beautiful picture of the Shepherd comforting His sheep with His presence, the rod of protection and the staff of guidance. Together, they illustrate God's closeness to His sheep, His authority and His loving kindness toward Christians. Your soul can rest assured in dark valleys because the Shepherd, the **One** who cares for *all* your soul needs, is with you.

REMEMBER GOD'S CHARACTER IN THE VALLEY

Wouldn't it be nice if life was a constant green pasture? But the pathway from one lush land to the next is always down the hillside, through the valley and back up the slope. A good shepherd understands it's a necessary journey because green pastures don't last forever. So he leads his sheep downward toward a better place.

It's in the valleys, where the sun is hidden, that anxiety rises up. It's hard to see or to believe a better place is ahead. **One might begin to doubt God in the darkness leaving a girl worried and afraid.** In Psalm 23:4, David makes a bold declaration, "I will not be afraid." David's confidence in dark valleys was grounded in his Shepherd.

But let's be honest, some dark valleys are like deep seas of blackness. During times of great anguish, broken relationships, sickness, depression or even death, making a bold declaration, like David, feels impossible. It takes faith in the valley to proclaim complete trust in the Shepherd. **One way to build your trust is to remember the provision of the Shepherd.**

1. Revisit what you've learned so far about the Shepherd's provision. Match the correct line of scripture with the correct provision in the box.

   1 The Lord is my shepherd;
      I have all that I need.
   2 He lets me rest in green meadows;
      he leads me beside peaceful streams.
   3 He renews my strength.
      He guides me along right paths,
         bringing honor to his name.
   4 Even when I walk
         through the darkest valley,
      I will not be afraid,
         for you are close beside me.
      Your rod and your staff
         protect and comfort me.

The Shepherd's Provision

- Rest for your soul
- Peace in your soul
- Guidance for your soul
- Contentment for your soul
- Strength in your soul
- Comfort for your soul

2. How might remembering God's provision help you when in a dark valley?

ACTS PRAYER

As you write your prayer consider what you have learned about Psalm 23.

Dear Lord,

Adoration

Give praise, honor, and glory to God for He is Lord over all.

I praise you because...

Confession

Repent, come clean & admit your sins, ask for forgiveness.

Forgive me for...

Thanksgiving

Recount your blessings & thank God for all He has done.

Thank you for...

Supplication

Make your requests, both for yourself and others. Ask God for what you need.

My requests are...

In Jesus' Name, Amen

"You prepare a feast for me in the presence of my enemies. You honor me by anointing my head with oil. My cup overflows with blessings."

PSALM 23:5

Week 6

Psalm 23

HE PROVIDES A FEAST

Generally speaking, most women like to plan or attend parties. Either way, I'm sure by now you've attended many celebrations. Whether it's your best friend's birthday bash, your sister's baby shower, your son's graduation or your husband's retirement commemoration, gathering together is enjoyable. A good party is one overflowing with "The Four F's" - family, friends, food and fun. But good parties don't happen by accident. A lot of planning and preparation precedes the best events. A good party begins with a good host.

A host is a person who welcomes and entertains guests in their home or at a designated venue. The host prepares for the guests by providing for their needs: food, beverages, a place to sit and entertainment. Every good host pays special attention to the individual needs of each guest by accommodating for food allergies and special needs. Each guest is well cared for because the host goes to great lengths to ensure a fun, satisfying and safe event.

In Psalm 23:5, David shifts the metaphor from a shepherd and his sheep to a host and his guest. The Shepherd, now the Divine Host, has prepared a feast. Before Him is a table filled with abundant provision and you are invited to come and enjoy. No host has ever planned and prepped better for your arrival than the Divine Host. He knows your deepest soul needs, after all, He created you (Genesis 1:26) and He knows your heart (Psalm 139:1). With great love He invites you to come and partake. He offers you spiritual food and drink to satisfy, sustain and strengthen your empty soul. Will you come to the table? Will you eat and drink what God has prepared for you?

SOUL NEED #5: A FEAST

Traits: An overflowing table filled with goodness. A banquet or celebration.

Struggle: Not hungry for God. Make my own table. Eating junk. Never satisfied.

Truth: The Shepherd (now the Host) provides an overflowing table filled with goodness that truly satisfies the soul.

NOT HUNGRY FOR GOD'S FEAST

David continues to describe his relationship with God. He begins verse five by painting a picture of a banquet table, *"You prepare a feast for me..."* (Psalm 23:5). David is the guest and God is the host. At God's table, God provides abundantly for David's needs. Everything God offers is spread out like a feast for David to come and enjoy.

Thanksgiving is the perfect image of a table overflowing with food. Just thinking about turkey, mashed potatoes, green beans, bread and pumpkin pie can cause a girl's tummy to growl! This kind of feast feeds the physical body while God's feast feeds the soul. God's spiritual table offers life, both now and forever, through believing in Jesus (John 6:51) and consuming the Word of God (Matthew 4:4).

Sometimes Christian women don't come to God's table to eat because they're not hungry for what God is offering. A girl might think, *"I know what's best for my life and I will feed myself."* Thoughts like this lead to trying to fill an empty soul with achievement, wealth, beauty or material items. Other times hunger for God is squashed by a busy schedule, the worries of life or consuming too much junk (social media, Netflix, gossip). Trying to fill inner longings with these types of things will never satisfy long term. The soul needs God and the eternal food He provides.

1. Just like eating junk food can interfere with your appetite for healthy food, so it is with your spiritual hunger for God. What kind of junk are you feeding your soul? How is it dulling your appetite for God?

EXAMINE CLOSELY

At the beginning of Psalm 23, David confidently declares, *"The LORD is my shepherd; I have everything I need"* (Psalm 23:1). The remainder of the Psalm supports why David lacks nothing. As you dig into the next section of Psalm 23 ask God to help you understand how He meets your needs so you can be as sure as David when you say, *"The LORD is my shepherd."*

Look at the Scripture and answer the questions below.

"You prepare a feast for me in the presence of my enemies.

You honor me by anointing my head with oil.

My cup overflows with blessings." Psalm 23:5 NLT

1. Underline any words that create a mental image. What pictures come to mind when you read this verse? Make notes below.

2. What human needs are represented in this verse?

3. Circle all the personal pronouns. Who are the personal pronouns referring to?

4. Put a box around the verbs. How do these verbs inform you about what is happening?

5. Summarize what you learned about the Shepherd who is describe as the Host.

THE THREE METAPHORS OF PSALM 23:5

Thousands of years ago David penned these words, *"You prepare a feast for me in the presence of my enemies. You honor me by anointing my head with oil. My cup overflows with blessings."* (Psalm 23:5). David was referring to God's provision during his lifetime and one might wonder what does this have to do with me today? Before you begin, remember Psalm 23 is a metaphor for David's relationship with God and it applies to us today. There are three images that represent spiritual truths about our relationship with God too - a feast, anointing oil and cup overflowing. Let's examine them below.

METAPHOR #1 - A FEAST

"You prepare a feast for me in the presence of my enemies..." Psalm 23:5.

The emphasis in this section of the verse is on the preparation and the host. The idea is that of a host inviting guests over and making everything ready for them. All the guests need to do is come, eat and enjoy. The Divine Host has invited you and me to come to His table, a table filled with daily blessings, spiritual blessings and provision that satisfy the hungry soul.

6. Read Ephesians 1:3-14 and list as many spiritual blessings as you can find.

7. Which spiritual blessing from your list above nourishes your soul the most? Why?

8. According to Ephesians 1:3, who are we to be united with in order to sit at God's table and enjoy His spiritual blessings?

9. What might "in the presence of my enemies" mean? (See Psalm 31:19)

METAPHOR #2 - ANOINTING OIL

"...You honor me by anointing my head with oil..." Psalm 23:5.

During biblical times it was customary for a host to welcome a guest into their home with a kiss, a drink, washing their feet and anointing their head with oil. Guests often arrived dirty and stinky from a long journey and without a shower for days. The anointing oil provided a soothing, healing effect and a perfume-like scent that refreshed the smell of the body. The sweet smell of a guest covered in oil is symbolic of the sweet smell of a Christian covered in the oil of the Holy Spirit.

10. What do you learn about the Holy Spirit? Match the verse with the correct verse address.

1. I Corinthians 6:19   • The Spirit lives in me.

2. I Corinthians 12:11   • The Spirit gives me spiritual gifts.

3. Ephesians 4:30   • The Spirit guarantees my salvation.

4. Romans 8:14   • The Spirit affirms I am God's child.

5. Romans 8:16   • The Spirit leads me.

6. John 16:13   • The Spirit guides me in all truth.

METAPHOR #3 - CUP OVERFLOWING

"...My cup overflows with blessings." Psalm 23:5.

The cup is a symbol used in the Bible literally and figuratively. In Psalm 23:5, the cup is a symbol of joy. God provided David with a feast and with anointing oil. God blessed David abundantly. Can you imagine David looking over all of God's provision, as his Shepherd and his Host, then saying, *"My cup overflows with blessing"* (Psalm 23:5)? It's as if David was counting his blessings and the result was joy. Joy overflowed because of God's love, care and provision.

11. What kind of life did Jesus come to give you? (See John 10:10)

HOW DO I EAT AT GOD'S TABLE?

You've been invited to sit and feast with God. He is the Divine Host who provides abundantly and gives your soul the nourishment it desperately longs for. His table offers rich foods filled with truth, life and blessing. But you must come and partake. Eating at God's table is consuming Scripture (Matthew 4:4). Your body needs fruits and vegetables but your soul needs the living Word of God.

But how do I consume God's Word? Consider eating a piece of watermelon. First, you prepare the watermelon for consumption by washing and cutting it. Then, you sink your teeth in to take a juicy bite. As you chew, you savor and enjoy the flavor. Finally, your body digests and absorbs all the good nutrients and vitamins in the watermelon. Metaphorically speaking, it's the same with the Bible and your soul. Consuming God's Word has four stages - preparing, eating, savoring and digesting.

Prepare

Just like you plan to eat three meals a day, schedule a daily time to eat your soul food. Also, think ahead about what you will consume - what book are you going to read? Are you reading through a book of the Bible or doing a Bible study? Make this decision in advance.

Eat

At meal time, you sit down, grab a fork and put the food in your mouth. Soul eating is opening your Bible, reading the text and putting the text in your mind and heart..

Savor

Some foods are so yummy you instinctively slow down to enjoy the smell and the taste. Reveling in the flavor makes it last longer. The Bible is yummy for your soul. Reading at a slower pace allows your soul to absorb all the flavor of what God is saying. Taking notice of the smells and tastes rather than chowing down will enrich mealtime.

Digest

Once mealtime is over your body continues to digest the food you've consumed. God's Word works the same way. Eating His Word is ingesting truth into your soul. When Bible eating time is over, the words still linger. But it's up to you to ponder and reflect upon them. His Word is living and active (Hebrews 4:12) and it continues to fuel your soul beyond mealtime.

1. Are you regularly coming to God's table to eat? What is one mealtime stage you can improve on: prepare, eat, savor or digest?

ACTS PRAYER

As you write your prayer consider what you have learned about Psalm 23.

Dear Lord,

Adoration
Give praise, honor, and glory to God for He is Lord over all.

I praise you because...

Confession
Repent, come clean & admit your sins, ask for forgiveness.

Forgive me for...

Thanksgiving
Recount your blessings & thank God for all He has done.

Thank you for...

Supplication
Make your requests, both for yourself and others. Ask God for what you need.

My requests are...

In Jesus' Name, Amen

"Surely your goodness and unfailing love will pursue me all the days of my life, and I will live in the house of the Lord forever."

PSALM 23:6

Week 7

HE PROVIDES GOODNESS & MERCY

Did you know counting your blessings is good for your soul? It's true! Giving thanks to God for all the good things He has given is like a river of hope flowing right through the insides of you. The Bible says when we pray and give thanks we will experience peace...a peace that is beyond human understanding (Philippians 4:7). A hopeful and peaceful soul is a satisfied and content soul. Before we move onto the final verse of Psalm 23, let's pause and give thanks for what we've already learned about the Shepherd's provision.

- Give thanks for He provides contentment (Psalm 23:1)

- Give thanks for He provides rest (Psalm 23:2)

- Give thanks for He provides direction (Psalm 23:3)

- GIve thanks for He provides comfort (Psalm 23:4)

- Give thanks for He provides a feast (Psalm 23:5)

As we conclude our study of Psalm 23 there are a few more provisions to add to the thankful list. The final Scripture says, *"Surely your goodness and unfailing love will pursue me all the days of my life, and I will live in the house of the LORD forever"* (Psalm 23:6). David recognizes a set of provisions - goodness & mercy (unfailing love). This duo works together...goodness to supply what you need and mercy to forgive you when you stray. David paints a picture of God chasing after him with His goodness and mercy. Then, the Shepherd provides for the soul's deepest longing - the desire for an eternal home. All the hills and valleys end with the Shepherd leading His sheep home to live with Him forever.

SOUL NEED #6: GOODNESS & MERCY

Traits: Loving kindess. Compassion. Forgivness.

Struggle: Doubt God's goodness and mercy in the dark valleys of life.

Truth: The Shepherd works all things out for good. Even in dark valleys, His goodness and mercy follow after His sheep, guiding them home.

DOUBTING GOD'S GOODNESS & MERCY

On the mountaintops it's easy to notice God's goodness and loving kindness, but what about in the dark valleys when everything is falling apart? It's often in the darkest moments of life that God seems to be the furthest away. The trials and challenges of the Christian woman's life are certainly tough. A toxic work environment, a negative pregnancy test for the fifteenth time, a wayward child, a stagnate marriage or a cancer diagnosis can leave a woman feeling depressed, anxious and alone. She might doubt God's goodness and love, thinking to herself, *"If God is good why is this happening to me?"* or *"If God loves me why can't I see Him or hear Him?"*

David was a man well aquatinted with dark valleys. Can you imagine being anointed as Israel's next king only to be hunted by the current reigning king? David experienced deep emotions while he was fleeing for his life (Psalm 57). His soul also suffered great anguish due to his sinful choices (Psalm 51). The pain of his sin covered his heart like a dark cloud. David could have doubted God but instead he wrote, *"Surely your goodness and unfailing love will pursue me all the days of my life..."* (Psalm 23:6). It's as if David was looking back over his life, and as he did, he noticed how God used his hilltops & his valleys for good.

God, who is good and merciful, uses your hilltops and valleys too. He causes everything in your life to work for your overall good (Romans 8:28). Nothing is wasted. Everything is used. Even the darkest of moments. The LORD, who began a good work in you is faithful to complete it (Philippians 1:6). His goodness and mercy chase after you every day of your life. You might not understand right now, but one day you'll look back and see how God worked it all out for your good.

1. Can you think of a difficult time when you didn't see God's goodness, but later you looked back and saw that He used it for your good?

EXAMINE CLOSELY

At the beginning of Psalm 23, David confidently declares, *"The LORD is my shepherd; I have everything I need"* (Psalm 23:1). The remainder of the Psalm supports why David lacks nothing. As you dig into the next section of Psalm 23 ask God to help you understand how He meets your needs so you can be as sure as David when you say, *"The LORD is my shepherd."*

Look at the Scripture and answer the questions below.

"Surely your goodness and unfailing love will pursue me all the days of my life, and I will live in the house of the Lord forever." Psalm 23:6 NLT

1. Underline any words that create a mental image. What pictures come to mind when you read this verse? Make notes below.

2. What human needs are represented in this verse?

3. Circle all the personal pronouns. Who are the personal pronouns referring to?

4. Put a box around the verbs? How do these verbs inform you about what is happening?

5. Summarize what you learned about the Shepherd.

CONFIDENCE IN THE LORD

David began the final verse of Psalm 23 solidifying his confidence in the Shepherd to supply all his needs. He said, *"Surely your goodness and unfailing love will pursue me all the days of my life..."* (Psalm 23:6). The word surely means only, absolutely, without a doubt and definitely. David wasn't saying occasionally, sometimes, only in the green pastures or by peaceful streams...he was convinced whatever the situation in life, the goodness and mercy of God was following him closely.

6. Above there are four alternative words for surely. Write one of them in the blank below.

" _____ your goodness and unfailing love will pursue me all the days of my life..." Psalm 23:6

7. How does substituting an alternative word deepen your understanding of this verse?

TWO SHEEPDOGS- GOODNESS & MERCY

Have you ever seen a sheepdog in action? They are amazing to watch! The sheepdog helps to gather or move a flock of sheep. While the shepherd leads from the front, the sheepdog pushes the flock forward from back. The sheepdog also prevents sheep from wandering and larger breeds protect the sheep from predators. The Shepherd of your soul has two sheepdogs following close behind you too. Their names are Goodness and Mercy and their job is to continually press you forward towards the Shepherd. When you wander, they steer you back home. On the hilltop and in the valley, Goodness and Mercy chase after you like a sheepdog pursues the sheep.

8. What do you learn about God's goodness? Match the verse with the correct verse address.

Goodness

1. Psalm 31:19
2. Psalm 107:8-9
3. Psalm 119:68
4. James 1:17

- All that is good is a gift from God.
- God satisfies the hungry & thirsty with good things.
- God is good and does only good.
- For those who fear Him, God's goodness is great.

9. What do you learn about God's mercy? Match the verse with the correct verse address.

Mercy

1. Psalm 86:5

2. Lamentations 3:22-23

3. Ephesians 2:4

4. Ephesians 2:5

- God is rich in mercy.

- God is ready to forgive; abounding in love.

- God's mercy never ends. It's new every morning.

- God's mercy makes us alive in Christ when we
  are dead in sin.

10. Look over what you learned about God's goodness and mercy. How does it make you feel to know, like sheepdogs, goodness and mercy follow you always?

THE SOUL'S GREATEST NEED - AN ETERNAL HOME

Set within the heart of every human being is the desire to live forever. The soul longs for eternity. The soul wants an eternal home. Psalm 23:6 ends with, *"...and I will live in the house of the LORD forever."* The Shepherd has provided your soul with an eternal dwelling place and it's called heaven.

11. What do you learn about heaven from the verses below?

- John 14:2-4

- John 14:6

- 2 Corinthians 5:1

- Philippians 3:20

- Revelation 21:3-8

12. What aspect of heaven does your soul long for the most?

DONT FORGET THE SHEPHERD

Psalm 23 is a personal psalm and is worth remembering for the rest of your life. On the hilltops and in the low valleys of life, reciting this psalm is good for your soul. The Shepherd longs to lead, comfort and protect you. He invites you to come to His table to eat and He pursues you with goodness and mercy. The Shepherd provides for all of your true soul needs including your deepest need for an eternal home. Commit to following Him all the days of your life. One day the pathway will take you to your forever home in heaven.

1. Write the missing personal pronouns in the blank spaces below. (I, me, my)

The Lord is _____ shepherd; _____ have all that need. He lets _____ rest in green meadows; He leads _____ beside peaceful streams. He renews _____ strength. He guides _____ along right paths, bringing honor to his name. Even when _____ walk through the darkest valley, _____ will not be afraid, for you are close beside . Your rod and your staff protect and comfort _____. You prepare a feast for _____ in the presence of _____ enemies. You honor _____ by anointing _____ head with oil. _____ cup overflows with blessings. Surely your goodness and unfailing love will pursue _____ all the days of life, and _____ will live in the house of the Lord forever.

2. Slowly read Psalm 23 above. Read it with confidence, faith and affection. Let the words soak into your soul. When you're done, answer the questions below.

- How does Psalm 23 make your soul feel? Why?

- What do you want to remember about the Shepherd of your soul?

Pray

ACTS PRAYER

As you write your prayer consider what you have learned about Psalm 23.

Dear Lord,

Adoration
Give praise, honor, and glory to God for He is Lord over all.

I praise you because...

Confession
Repent, come clean & admit your sins, ask for forgiveness.

Forgive me for...

Thanksgiving
Recount your blessings & thank God for all He has done.

Thank you for...

Supplication
Make your requests, both for yourself and others. Ask God for what you need.

My requests are...

In Jesus' Name, Amen

The Plan of Salvation

GOD LOVED YOU FIRST

Regardless of how you may feel (unworthy, shameful or not good enough) God loves you. His love is not dependent upon you because He loved you first. This love is revealed to us through Christ's birth, life, death and resurrection. Christ, although perfect himself, died on the cross and paid the price for the sins of all people. God offers you forgiveness. And by Christ's resurrection God offers the promise of eternal life. While Christ died and rose again for everyone, He comes to you personally...as an individual to establish a personal relationship with you. To accept His offer of forgiveness and eternal life, you must respond to Him.

REVEALING GOD'S LOVE FOR YOU

God loves you today...exactly as you are. He longs to be in a close relationship with you...to bless you, strengthen you and give you an abundant life. His offer is not only for here on earth but also for eternal life with Him in Heaven.

"For God so loved the world, that he gave his only Son, so that everyone who believes in Him will not perish but have eternal life." John 3:16

MANKIND'S SINFUL NATURE

Not one single human is perfect. Every one of us falls short, and when we acknowledge this truth, we can clearly see our separation from God. God is holy and we are not.

"All have sinned; all fall short of God's glorious standard." Romans 3:23

SIN HAS A PRICE

The price of sin is spiritual death and ultimately, eternal separation from God. BUT, with God's free gift, we can receive a pardon for our sin and provision for eternal life.

"For the wages of sin is death, but the free gift of God is eternal life through Christ Jesus our Lord." Romans 6:23

CHRIST PAID THE PRICE

The price of sin is spiritual death and ultimately, eternal separation from God. BUT, with God's free gift, we can receive a pardon for our sin and provision for eternal life. Many people believe that doing good, charitable acts will make God love you. Not true. Even in your sin...God loves you. There is nothing that we can do to make God love us or to earn His love. God sent His Son to take your place and pay the price for your sin while you were still a sinner. Why? So you can be reconciled to Him.

"But God showed His great love for us by sending Christ to die for us while we were still sinners."
Romans 5:8

REDEMPTION IS A FREE GIFT

God's special favor or grace means getting what you don't deserve. By God's grace He offers you what you are unable to do for yourself - salvation and eternal life with Him. Receive and believe... that's it! With all of your heart believe that Christ died for you...to deliver you from sin and to give you eternal life.

"God saved you by His special favor when you believed. And you cannot take credit for this; it is a gift from God. Salvation is not a reward for good things we have done, so none of us can boast about it."
Ephesians 2:8-9

YOU MUST ACCEPT CHRIST

To become a child of God, you must receive Him and accept what He has done for you. Jesus Christ is standing at the door of your heart inviting you in...BUT, you must receive Him.

"But to all who believe in Him and accept Him, He gave the right to become children of God."
John 1:12

ARE YOU READY TO RECEIVE HIM NOW?

You can invite Christ into your heart and life right now by simply praying this prayer:

Dear Lord, I know that I am a sinner and that I need your forgiveness. I believe that Jesus Christ died in my place to take the penalty for my sin and that He rose from the dead. Right now, I invite Jesus to come into my heart and to be my Savior. Thank you for creating me and making a way for me. Help me to learn and grow in the knowledge of your love so that I may please You in every part of my life. In Jesus' name, Amen.

Facilitating a Small Group

I'm sure you have heard your pastor say more than once, "join a group" and that's because within groups our learning and growing potential expands. Together we feel known, heard and accepted, and we gain valuable new insights from each other.

Gathering a group of women who want to grow closer to God while experiencing connection and support takes a step of faith. By starting your own small group you are opening a space where women can experience community while deepening their relationship with the Lord.

How do I start a small group?

If you feel a nudge in your heart to start a small group begin by praying. God might already be prompting your heart, but it's always wise to check in with Him first. Then, when you are ready to proceed, follow these steps:

- Gather a group of women. It could be women from church, your next-door neighbors, or if you are a mom of a teen girl, you could invite other moms with teen girls and make it a mother/daughter Bible study. For a mom and teen girls group, the girls need a copy of *Psalm 23 for Teen Girls* and moms need a copy of *Psalm 23 for Women*. If you need help, reach out at hello@jjgutierrezauthor.com. I would love to offer support, guidance and encouragement along the way.
- Pick a start date, day of the week, time and location. Keep in mind you will need 8 weeks to complete the study: Opening week and 7 weeks for each chapter.
- Call or send an email and invite any girls you think might be interested at least 2-3 weeks in advance.
- All participants, including the leaders need:

  - The book: *Psalm 23 for Women*

  - A physical Bible

  - Pen/pencil

What makes a good facilitator?

A facilitator is simply a person who is willing to lead the discussion about each chapter. She aids in the process of helping participants learn from their own experiences and shared information. A good facilitator will follow a few simple guidelines:

- Respecting the time of the group by starting and ending on time
- Giving everyone in the group an equal opportunity to share
- Not allowing the discussion to become advice giving or counseling
- Staying away from giving your opinion about some else's situation
- Creating a safe and trusted environment where girls can share honestly
- Staying focused on the intended discussion and lesson
- Adding fun ice breakers to the beginning of each meeting (see discussion questions)
- Celebrating at the end with a potluck or a dessert bar

I am excited you are considering starting a small group! It's been my experience whenever I step out in faith to lead a group God reveals Himself to me in new and amazing ways, and I am confident you will experience that too. But also beware that the enemy may try to attack you with fear or second guessing your ability to lead. He certainly doesn't want anyone helping other girls grow closer to God by digging into His Word. Instead of becoming discouraged, consider it confirmation that you are courageously doing exactly what God has planned.

Opening Discussion Questions

Getting Started - Gather your group for introductions. Make sure everyone has a copy of *Psalm 23 for Women*. You can have the group members order their book ahead of time or you can order them yourself and hand them out. Always start with introductions and an ice breaker to get eveyone feeling comfortable. Below are discussion questions to help you begin each meeting. You don't need to ask every question. Pick 1-2 per Bible study class. For the introduction week, read the introduction together. Review when and what time you meet and what the expectations are. Is everyone completing their study at home or are you completing it together? For weeks 1-7, complete the Bible study either by reviewing eveyone's answers or by doing the study together.

Discussion Questions: Introduction week

- What is your greatest need?
- What is contentment?
- What is your soul?

Discussion Questions: Week 1

- What is your favorite song and why?
- What are different categories or genres of music?
- Do you know what a psalm is?
- What do you know about Psalm 23?
- Do you know who King David was?

Discussion Questions: Week 2

- What are some of your basic needs?
- Who do you rely on to supply your basic needs?
- What kind of things do you want or need?
- Do you know what a shepherd does?
- Can you imgaine not wanting anything? What would it be like?

Discussion Questions: Week 3

- Do you like to go to bed or are you a night owl?
- Is it easy for you to fall asleep or do you struggle?
- What kind of things keep your soul from resting?
- Describe an earthly peaceful place. What makes it peaceful to you?

Discussion Questions: Week 4

- Have you ever gotten lost? What did it feel like to be lost?
- Are you stubborn? Do you insist on doing things your own way?
- What does it mean to follow God?

Discussion Questions: Week 5

- When life is difficult, who gives you comfort? What does this person do that makes you feel comforted?
- Can you remember a time you were afraid of the dark? What happened?
- What are some common dark valleys that most people go through?
- Do you think the Christian life is one free of hardship and challenges?

Discussion Questions: Week 6

- If you were at a feast, what foods would you want at the table?
- Have you ever hosted a party? What did you do as the host?
- Can you remember a party with a good host? A bad host? What was the difference between the two experiences?
- Do you enjoy reading God's Word? Why or why not?
- Do you regularly consume God's Word? Why or why not?

Discussion Questions: Week 7

- As you look back on your life, do you recall a situation when you felt God's goodness?
- What causes you to doubt God's goodness?
- What comes to mind when you think of heaven?

FOR MORE INFORMATION ABOUT

JJ Gutierrez

SPEAKER - TEACHER - AUTHOR

WAYS TO CONNECT AT:
www.jjgutierrezauthor.com, @instagram.com/jjgutierrezauthor, hello@jjgutierrezauthor.com

If you enjoyed this book, please consider leaving a review on Amazon. Reviews make a big difference. They help to get resources like this into the hands of other women.

ADDITIONAL BOOKS BY JJ GUTIERREZ

FOR WOMEN OF ALL AGES & STAGES

FOR TEEN GIRLS

Moms of teen girls can study together but with their tailor made books!

FOR POLICE WIVES AND POLICE KIDS

   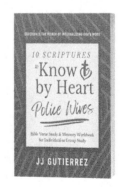

"Your Word is a lamp to my feet and a light to my path."

Psalm 119:105

143

Made in the USA
Las Vegas, NV
04 January 2025

15707041R00039